Tales of a hopeless romantic

Emma Harris

BookLeaf Publishing

India | USA | UK

Presentation by *BookLeaf Publishing*

Web: www.bookleafpub.com

E-mail: info@bookleafpub.com

ISBN: 9789358316490

First edition 2023

DEDICATION

To my family, you are my home

Brown eyed girl

The moon winks, a lovers satin smile,
failing to light up sunken steps
Such a sorrowful sight, the girl with the brown
eyes
Cheeks swell salty red, whispers stolen with
thought.
She wonders if she could possibly look like one
of the girls from the movies
cherry lipped and locks of mousy brown.
If you cannot be a doe eyed damsel, why be
anything at all?
Hiding beneath sweeping black lashes
fearful of catching his eye
It would be a shame for him to steal her breath
away again

The touch of love

Is this how I die?
By her gentle hand.
Skin against skin, I shiver
Her knuckles push against blade, skin tearing
between ribs
I cannot find it in me to push her off
I surrendered to her touch long ago.
She looks so beautiful, even with my blood on
her face.
Blood blends with flushed cheeks and tears
drown with rain.
We did seem to always find our way together
She is sorry, why is she sorry?
Does she not enjoy the feeling of my beating
heart?
I fade deeper into night, death surprisingly
sweet.
I soak further into skin, how difficult i shall be
to wash out.
No sound, no noticeable change in the air, i
disappear the softest whisper.

Cramp

Cramp, I mask with my bones
You have me share my skin
Stretch my soul to translucent tissue paper
Do you love me more like this?
You swipe greedy for beats of flesh
Love is not meant to leak from your eyes
I strip my skin to patch up your pain
Cramp, I find you, in the loss of myself

Scent

Duvet soaked in synthetic chamomile
still too weak to disguise his trace
Tobacco and soft vanilla
Lured cotton between fingers
trapped with the memory of him
Of course the sun continued to shine through the
landing
However, she could no longer seem to feel it

Grey

Such a blessed occasion, man and woman inside
crumbled church.
He reminds her of the colour grey
the one she splatted on empty walls
Bland and pasty, a thick sheet of soiled white
The true epitome of everything plain
He was the antithesis of how she imagined a
prince.
He was not a dashing amber.
Would he see in shades of grey?
Would he speak in black or white?
Disappointment soaked her bones
She drowned into skin of lace.
Hands joined in union, the clock a thief of time
He looked at her in more then colour
For he looked at her in feeling.
The unspoken possibility of a new beginning.
Something more grey then a simple
arrangement.
A crafted promise of a life of wild, passionate
grey
Painting more than just her room
Consuming her completely
So much more then grey

Afterlife

This is what being young feels like
it feels like you are swinging
watching the grass hopper that flew
cuddles from your mother
who wears mainly green and blue

How it ends

We had different movie taste
In fact, we had different taste in everything
i realise now why i hated his movies
the ending was not quick like we were
when moments end in reality, its as quick as a
pulse and as forgetful as a meal
His movies ended in length, in pain and
heartache
I wished our ending could have stretched as far
The same way my skin stretched beneath his
hands

Universe

I'm lucky I did not have to search to find you
I'm lucky I was born knowing you
I would find you in every life time
and smile at you in every room

Orange

A segment of my orange for all of you
you are sweeter then all the times before
riper then what i had known to be love
I wish you had tried me when i was softer
time seems to have left my roots bitter

Girlhood

If you love something a small part of it will
always stay
I am always going to be here
in this exact moment, on this exact day, at this
exact time
My jaw hurts from grinning
I am so lucky you are my best friend
I know that this moment will live on, long after
we have left

Poison

He wished he could cocoon himself in her
laughter
suffocate himself in her touch
he wanted to choke to her spontaneous jokes
But he only tasted blood in his mouth
She welcomes him with open arms
chaos and tranquillity in one
The moonlight watched the sway of
entanglement
Soothing with the breeze and the damp sand on
his skin
Now he only dances with her shadow

Mornings

I woke up yesterday
Your hand in my hair
Do you remember how much i love you?
Sincerely, faithfully, now

Naive

Is it conceited if I try and act older?
I am conflicted and ashamed
I swear I can change
I'll write with my finger the words i cannot say
to you
The glass damp against my print

Blue eyed boy

You feel like light
that shines upon my smile
and i smile so wide at you it blocks the shade
I realise i have not felt like this in a while
and fate praises the choice it made

For you

I feel whole and warm, my heart flutters and I
cannot think
I do not need to think when i can listen
listening to you is nearly as beautiful as the
green hidden in your iris
Your eyes speak a thousand words and even
more stories
Your still so young yet life has not been easy
Still, there is beauty in your battles and warmth
in your history
Can I kiss you until your doubts disappear?
Let me speak your worth into your lips and
remind you that you are it for me
You are beautifully brave and tremendously
charismatic
the world is not your oyster but your paper
Let me take away the fear of what comes later

Reincarnation

I have always been skeptical of reincarnation
Searching again for what I once held
Having to yearn for what I loved so dearly
The thought is daunting
Or perhaps it is because i was yet to find my
person
The person I would search for in every life time
The one who's soul is half of mine
and smile i would seek in a crowded room
Searching for you is the hardest thought to
conquer
I pray the other half of me senses we have met
before

Taking flight

I hope you know you hurt me
you turned my body inside out with fever
What I thought was love was devoured by
realism
I escape with the desire to be clean
You loved me tragically
I do not think it was love at all

Temptation

She was cupids bow, sharp in posture
Tempting like Aphrodite in cloth
She felt like the prettiest hell he had been in
He knows he would chose to stay

Liar

I dream here
the fragmented memory of us
I must have buried my trust around here
oh how i burn

Healing

You touch me so tenderly
I did not realise my wounds until now
for I formed scabs on the inside
not visible to the eye
I feel they may peel away
with every kiss of yours
I am becoming softer

Showers

Water in my eyes, never felt so good
I know you are smiling, even with my eyes
closed
I could find you in the dark, my lover
May we bathe in the moment of warmth
and forget everything else for a while

www.ingramcontent.com/pod-product-compliance
Lightning Source LLC
LaVergne TN
LVHW050849200726
843508LV00013B/2995